Michigan Farmhouse
Naming the Rooms

To Jane:
for the love of poetry,
Barbara
Oct 15, 1995

Barbara Esch Shisler

Michigan Farmhouse:
Naming The Rooms
© 1994 by Barbara Esch Shisler

Photos:
Jacob Esch—cover
GiGi Malinchak—East Room
Marilyn Nolt—North Room and South Room
Harold Shisler—West Room

Design:
The Creative Network (cover & section pages)

Consulting Editors:
Janet, Jeff, Lois, Mary Lou, Ruth, & Mary

ISBN: 0-9634083-7-2

Library of Congress Catalogue
Card Number: 94-65917

Printed in the United States

Published by
Ryanna Books
P.O. Box 1512
Richmond, IN 47375
317-966-4519

My Michigan farmhouse faced north so squarely that I never questioned directions. I knew, even at the age of five, that a half mile east and one mile south would take me to my two room country school of Winsor.

Life has never been so clear since. In Pennsylvania the roads meander every which way and houses snuggle in hills and woods with never a sign of alignment with the rest of the world. But I will always carry with me those compass-like rooms and the perspectives they engendered.

Barbara Esch Shisler
Telford, PA
1994

TO MY BROTHERS AND SISTERS
who were shaped by the same rooms
in ways different from my own
but just as truly,
I dedicate this book:
RUTH, CLAIR, JANET, JOAN, and KEITH

The following poems first appeared in these publications:

"Utterance"   *Born Giving Birth: creative*
                         expressions of Mennonite
                         women [Faith And Life Press]

"Baby"   *Christian Century*

"Boundaries"   *Christian Living*
"At The Bloodmobile"
"Canning Peaches"

"Year Of The Buckwheat" *Creeping Bent*

"The Book"   *Festival Quarterly*

"Father"   *Gospel Herald*
"The Groundhog"
"Through A Glass Less Darkly"
"Time Enough"

"Janice"   *Hiriam Poetry Review*

"Faithless At The Shore" *The Other Side*
"Yes All Day"
"Roar From The Wilderness"

"When Will We Be Sisters?" *Sojourners*

"green of the way"   *Stone Country*

"I Believe In The   *A Widening Light: Poems of the*
    Resurrection"   *Incarnation* [Harold Shaw Publi-
                         shers]
"Poem For Easter"

Contents

Michigan Farmhouse 13

I
North Room
Collecting The World's Chill

Grief Eating 17
Ruin 19
When Will We Be Sisters? 21
Likenesses 23
Death 25
Cleaning Toilets For The Mentally Retarded 27
Baby 29
The Book 31

II
South Room
Basking In Pink Flannel

Canning Peaches 35
Love Poem At 50 37
High School Reunion 39
Convergence 41
At The Bloodmobile 43
Canyon de Chelly 45
The Groundhog 47
Father 49

III
East Room
Mirroring The Mystery

green of the way 53
To The Woods 55
The Power Meeting 57
Janice 59
Year Of The Buckwheat 61
Back In My Room 63
I Believe In The Resurrection 65
Poem For Easter 67
Yes All Day 69

IV
West Room
Shoving Off

Going Down Cellar 73
Time Enough 75
Faithless At The Shore 77
Roar From The Wilderness 79
Boundaries 81
Hawk 83
Through A Glass, Less Darkly 85
Utterance 87

About the Author 89

Michigan Farmhouse
Naming The Rooms

Michigan Farmhouse

Awakened at 3 A.M. by alarms of endings—
I fall into my childhood home
squared North to South, East to West,
its rooms named and kept;
the smell of bed and cupboard,
bloom of sunrise, furrow of death.

The North Room names Grandfather
laid like a field, his hand cold as
Michigan ground before the thaw.
His face steams with tears,
my mother's breath batters his chest;
Thin against her dress,
I collect the world's chill.

South above the kitchen smells of supper,
I kneel at the register warming my face.
Christmas Eve, and parents pile gifts
at our plates, candy and fruit,
covered white with the Sunday tablecloth.
My eyes press, ecstasy is my name
basking in pink flannel.

Behind French doors of the East Room
my mother slept, my father waked
to pear trees and sunrise,
bed of conception and birth,
my sidelong stare; the dresser
of my mother's things precious, fragile,
and myself mirroring the mystery.

From the West window I color in
a tree and rock, artlessly grand;
the tree seeks clouds, the rock
for children shoving each other off,
and the push on the bike
to wallow down the lane
until scabbed and scarred
we head to the far horizon.

From peaks and eaves
to the cave of cellar
a child fleshed her soul.
Home of endings, beginnings.

I

North Room

Collecting the World's Chill

Grief Eating

Pull up a chair and sit down.
Wait. It will come,
course after course.
There is plenty. Don't be afraid to take.

Birth, shuddering rupture,
leaving home for the first time
with nothing but your skin
against the cold and clamor,
bruising edges, rude light.
Soon you know life is a grief
and you are a sigh,
a catch in the throat
without bearings any direction.

Then you start school
and loneliness breathes down your back,
stupidity squats in your chair,
a million eyes counting
how many you get wrong.

But life goes on: marriage-grief, mother-
grief, menopause. Come, pass your plate,
there is plenty more.
Chew slow. Swallow well.
These griefs nourish by entering the blood.
Mourned, they will make you strong.
They will charge your bones
with the power of marrow.

Ruin

In the chlorine-clean locker room at the Y,
a company of elderly women
mingle gently as they dress,
oblivious to ravage and to me,
trying at forty to swim,
ashamed as a girl on the examining table
of the doctor's office.

I bathed my mother
in the slow ruin of her heart;
dried her cream-white skin,
smoothed her dark and heavy hair,
never spoke of beauty
never mentioned death.

I play Russian Roulette
standing before the mirror
to check things out.
(so far so good
especially when the light's right.)

Last night sitting with friends,
a med student telling a cadaver joke,
and everyone laughing,
I held my hand to my face,
felt my teeth and mouth part,
my jaw shift at my skull
like a house tilting.

When Will We Be Sisters?

Now is my year of my mother's age,
the one death caught her at and froze,
catching too the foot-tapping, finger-
drumming daughter of the final photograph.
But this year I'm her equal, a delayed twin,
same name, same birthday,
and bell-clanging same age.
Were she to come back she'd think me
eighteen, and warn me about the world.
She wouldn't believe I've been wise as she
and know more about raising children.
But maybe she's been learning too-
finding images, exploring stars,
unraveling Revelation.
Maybe we could talk of Hopkins,
and what's in outer space,
and when the world will end,
and still, she'd teach me a thing or two.
Maybe we could explain ourselves-
why she cried and I turned cold,
what I concealed and she suspected-
explain ourselves, and turn to sisters.

Likenesses

I was skinny like her,
In a rush, done too soon,
Crumbs missed, corners left;

I was skimpy like her,
Nickels gripped, snippets saved,
Finding the cheapest in the five and dime;

I was common like her,
Dull to what goes, what's nice,
The merit of polish.

I was my grandmother's likeness.
Like my mother in not liking
the likeness; like my mother
in name and date of birth;
Like my mother in the meaning of our names.

Like my mother in the
Stranger of our names.

Death

Death
goes for the bone.
Shears what's loose.
Hones the edge.
Death's gimlet
goes to the core,
thinner
air,
barer
view.

High
overhead
Death takes to the wire
as all eyes follow
his trim
taut
hold,
his
prim
tapered
toes.

Death bows,
deft prince,
to his prize.

Cleaning Toilets For
The Mentally Retarded

They are not grateful.
Only the Board of Health
and the Supervisor take note.
They are oblivious to bacteria,
smudging themselves as cheerily
as they do the bathroom;
defecating, an absorbing business,
even for geniuses.

Gladys giggles at her 4 A.M. game
rolling paper into softballs,
playing plug the sewer
and flood the floor.

It is fitting for a poet to clean
toilets of the profoundly fated,
evoking Auden's observation,
" . . . for poetry makes nothing happen."

My sister polishes her coffee table,
an antique commode, walnut-rich,
serving sweets into my hands.
I attend to toilets
and uncommon souls rolling softballs,
and my own appointment with a fate
that moves through me without purpose,
without praise.

Baby

In Longwood Gardens
we laugh at the ugly baby
lolling like a roll of fat
around her mother's neck.

No one minds the lack of class,
least of all, the baby.

Some day when she suspects
she will pretend
and conceal.

The instant she knows
herself,
Paradise is over.

The Book

The book would be blue, his dream
spent, he knew which to choose
Sunday morning when the lot*
would fall on God's elected.
The sweet hot joy wet his throat,
but he swallowed; no man dared
to speak the word inviting vanity.
He cast his eyes in silence to the floor.

The congregation, a field behind him
that sighed and rustled like his corn ready
to reap; the three on the front bench bowed
and the prayers of the people pried
the heavy air. He raised his eyes
to the word that waited, blue,
and went first to the table and returned-
himself, too, an opened, empty book.

He wept, no one knew why
nor would, when the Bishop kissed
God's Chosen. He embraced his brother
and went home to his corn,
no man was a better farmer,
turning worn ground into fields of gold;
and late at night he sat and read
from a black book. He owned none blue.

*a religious practice in which the book containing a slip of paper
revealed God's will for a new minister

II

South Room
Basking in Pink Flannel

Canning Peaches

Why can peaches
when I could be writing poems?
I yearn for health,
red-gold flesh stinging
the tongue, syruping the soul,
jarring the mind's juices.
I say to my Love,
"Let us feast on a sphere,
suck honey to heal our hurt,
thistles have turned velvet,
winter to engorged bloom."
I weigh in each hand
these measures, life-ripe;
Why write poems
when I could be canning peaches?

Love Poem At 50

Early to bed on my birthday,
and I feel the teeth of an ache,
a bite in the belly
nibbling down my legs.
Then the stream
on schedule for 38 years
with time out decades ago
for our cheerful progeny.

If only I could turn ova
into poems, I'd open a nursery,
attend each pink breath and toenail
with the brow of a madonna.

Scientists say that women who
inhale male odor menstruate longer.

How long, husband, will we celebrate
this rich, ungarnered yield,
your scent nurturing
our warm and love-wet bed?

High School Reunion

On the third floor of the Hampton Inn
we roll on the kingly bed,
I giddy about tomorrow, and
our 35-year class reunion.

"Are you the same person you were in '54?"
I chortle against his shoulder,
tasting the skin of our aging love.
"Yes," he shrugs without wonder,
while I giggle more madly,
"Am I the same person I was in '54?"

The limp memory of graduation
swells like a hot balloon
spurting orange energy
that lifts me blue heavenward.

Life was love, and love was you,
and in the Hampton Inn I hang on tight
having come from what we were
to wondering who we are.

Convergence

We make our way upstream,
shape a V on hearing a summons.
Creatures, we head toward a place
draped in white or black
as planes or trains or turnpikes
take us to the eye of events
where love and death clutch
our hands and collect us
in a dense and tenuous circle.

How new the old of my sister's face.
How old the system of blood
arching back, reaching forward,
keeping our pulse, converging
through our mute and babbling hearts.

At The Bloodmobile

In my wavering I will do this deed,
climb on the table and be tapped,
a maiden oil field,
though this oil is dearer than Iran
and the color of love.
I study the ceiling, pine cathedral arch,
knots like clots, while the nurse cheers,
"Running nicely!"

Blood scenes spurt before me:
Calvary's fountain with plunging sinners;
Sticky white underwear and thirteen's
frenzied joy;
The drenched fur of a wayside kitten;
Sacred streams of birth and death,
while here mine darkly
fattens a plastic bag.

In company my heart pumps on.
Laid out in rows, we bleed for mankind.
Pure-blood, blue-blood,
we sacrifice our true-blood,
rubies offered for the mining
to save the world its deadly dying.

My oblation ended, I rise to tea
and doughnuts, party Red Cross,
abashed for my blushing pint.

Save valor for the fight,
puncture vainglory,
laugh at a bleeding heart.
Go refreshed into summer dark,
into rich dark life lean and pulsing.

Canyon de Chelly

Column of deliberation,
Spider Rock rises,
boundaried in thousand foot cliffs
of gold and rose, cream, vermillion.

Rock is a word that stands for itself.

Spider Rock names Holy Spider Woman,
weaving teacher to hogan people.
From her door, a deep-eyed weaver
studies the light on the canyon walls,
shimmer and pale, shade and glow,
and knows like her loom,
life with the Rock.
Sheep bells quiver in canyon stillness,
a small garden waits for rain.
The dust-colored hogan
nestles under blazing sandstone frescoes.

Rock is a word that moves with itself
in the rhythm of a mother's arms,
the comfort of a swaying body,
the baby nodding on her back.

We are the Rock's children,
sings the Navajo.
We are sons and daughters of the Rock.

The Groundhog

Blessed is the groundhog,
his name is Meek.
Bundling through the ditches
he shuns publicity,
at home in the womb of the ground.
His belly swells
in the fat of the meadow,
in innocence he mistakes our gardens,
defenseless to dog and gun.

Self-image is not his charge,
he flees his frame,
from the shadow
of his winter shape
and seasoned, appears
to the ready world,
upright, the creature confirmed.

Blessed is the groundhog,
True inheritor of the earth.

Father

The March snow I've been waiting for.
I lie in bed listening to pins prickling
the window, thinking of my 88-year-old father
tending his garden miles and miles away.
His snow peas six feet high, he writes,
and turnips sweet and crisp as apples.
I see him, hardy as a gnome,
white fringe fluffed under a John Deere cap,
hands fathering his green exuberant plot.
At noon in his kitchen he cooks potatoes,
turnips, and onions, spreads peanut butter toast
to rejoice in his dinner, his round head bowed
in whispered praise, his blessing raised and raining
on his 52-year-old child, miles and miles away.

III

East Room
Mirroring the Mystery

green of the way

The Royal Realm Begins Someplace Here
And Entering Forest Shadow
I keep An Eye Peeled, An Ear
Cocked, Leaving The Blinding Meadow
Of Beetle And Nettle And Heat.

But Having Scrutinized The Trees,
Overturned Rocks, Interrogated Bird And Deer,
Left A Bullet In The Jaw Of A Bear,
I Crash Furious Into Failure,
Damn Same Name, No Banner, Nothing New.

     the royal realm begins someplace here
     and entering forest shadow
     i keep an eye peeled, an ear
     cocked, leaving the blinding meadow
     of beetle and nettle and heat.

     and having bared my white feet
     feel the ground, put on the green
     of the way, gather boughs for a bed.
     why kneeling to free a spider from a stream,
     why thorns like a crown at my head?

To The Woods

It's like that hunger
that isn't really hunger;
You've eaten and aren't fed.
The gnaw wants more.
But not bread.

It's like that yearning
that wants tears but none come;
Drought shrivels the air,
deviling your eyes, burning.

Perhaps if I go to the woods
and sit by a stream,
listen to the towhee's call
and smooth my hands with a stone,
Perhaps the smell of death there,
the upward thrust of a bloodroot bud
will heal the hollow of being human,
the aching desire for someone other.

The Power Meeting

It does not matter much that tonight in Washington
prime minds pragmatize;
It is of small regard that in Hollywood
gold images are hugged all suave and shine;
Even Tokyo blades cutting economic cream pies
and Oxford pipes wafting rationales world-wise
do not undo the brows of three gray sisters
and two portly brothers at their meeting
in Souderville.

Hands bountifully Bibled, they knit a circle,
unfold old pages, trace the promises.
Hearts gather scattered threads
grievously severed.
Prayer kindles their lips, warm
on the backs of chairs,
mellowing the room.
They arouse the voice of a hymn
and go tenderly home
humming the refrain:
"There is Pow'r in the Blood of the Lamb."

Janice

The moon is round as a clock.
Janice rises from her bed,
her bed of broken shell,
of salted crests,
of cold dashed rock,
to navigate the halls.
Again. Again.

"To bed, Janice,"
I tell her,
and channel her in,
her squat woman body and baby brain
slip through
as simply as a fish.

I close the door
to a squall of laughter.
The moon rinses her hair.

Year Of The Buckwheat

Corn and beans paled
in the garden of thinning soil,
the years gone stonily gray
until the summer of buckwheat.
The plowed ground sprawled,
blind and dumb. Clouds creased their brows.
I thrust my hands full of kernels
and splashed the dim dust
as the sky let loose and fell in pools.

Earth turned; buds burgeoned
round as high notes, splattered wide
and white as bees came yodeling in droves,
the sun leaped through green
and sang to the thickening beneath.

Tonight under a full moon
the buckwheat is a still white sea.
I dream.
You and I drift to it,
our blood in bloom,
where we lie down together
to receive such joy
as could recreate the world.

Back In My Room

Light breaks suddenly behind my eyes.
I open and the room is lit,
white morning among the green leaves,
my plants, like sisters, stirring at my side,
O'Keefe's RED HILLS gleaming the wall,
my body, my self, quiet in my bed,
the blankets snuggling me like hugs
in the soft deep comfort of safe-at-home.

Last week, leaving this room for the hospital
in the pre-dawn dark, cancer like a goon
waving his gun at my head, I tremble
with the unknown, the scalpel, the surgeon's hand
rummaging, my pale belly stunned.
What is diseased is removed.
I wake, pained and dizzy,
to the news that the cancer is gone. I will be well.
I will go home to rest in this sunny room.

Tears flood my face. I lift my hands
to a Trinity of Thou's: Lover, Healer, Quickener.
You breathe this room bright with life, light with joy.
My heart breaks. My soul sings.

I Believe In The Resurrection

What chance at apostleship have I,
mouthing the creed, buried deep
in blankets, dreading the day.
I clutch the dark, the sweet
oblivion of sleep, its cushioned coma.
Dawn nudges night,
finding stones and dispensing orders
while I cling to my crypt
as though I hadn't heard
where the power is, or that deathwishes
are doomed, or that day's
determined light
will raise me, wide-eyed.

Poem For Easter

Rise, daffodil,
against the stones
that shall yield
to your yellow vow.

Rise, onion shoot,
from an odious shroud
to green exclamation;
your death is done!

Rise, children
of the winter mind,
run to the garden
and kneel to the sun.

Yes All Day

"Say yes."

Yes, I say, obeying the command,
O.K., yes, and reach for the light, throwing
off the covers, and meeting the floor
with shuddering feet.
And it's yes all day,
yes, saying no to dark webs clutching,
no to the spectre of missiles stalking,
no to sludge for body and soul,
no to ennui, no to no.

And it's yes all day as the music summons
and every nuance peals like a bell,
and every tint has a hint of green,
the touch on my skin,
the taste on my tongue.
It's yes all day as NO falls stricken
by the spellbound stone that's heaved aside,
It's yes in reply to tone and timbre,
the dazzling gardener calling my name,
in the yes of alpha, the yes of omega,
the yes that's a yes to the sun going down.

IV

West Room
Shoving Off

Going Down Cellar

What farmer's child,
sent for a jar of supper fruit,
hasn't been tried by the devil
the minute she leaves the stairs.

She creeps toward the cistern,
black water nudging at cracks;
She climbs and peeks at the shiny eye
that stares back
promising a cold drowning.
A furnace of bloated limbs and heaving gut
bellows the tale of a little girl
who put wood to its mouth,
her apron lit, her eyes fried.
The pump salivates; its open jaw grinds
and grabs at the skirt she clutches
as she leaps for the fruit cellar door
that cries alarm to mice and potatoes
squirming in the dark.
She seizes the string and light dazzles
the shelves; she gathers gold and red
to her ribs; scuttles to the kitchen's kingdom
and her mother's face. Around the table
the family hands the glowing bowl
to take and eat.

Time Enough

In that blank second between fastening the seat belt
and reaching for the ignition,
or the moment facing the bathroom mirror
with the water running cold to warm;
During that split space after a cat screams,
and you don't know whose,
or the dark page before
the television show comes on,
there is time to hear
life's most pressing question.

During the interval waiting for the butter
to be passed,
or the number dialed
and the voice that says hello;
In that stillness between a nose tingle
and the relieving sneeze,
or the pause made by your hand cupped
reaching for your change,
there is time enough
to say Yes or No.

Faithless At The Shore

Scowling I rub off the sand,
the salt and sweat
to hurry inland, my
annual homage paid.

The Sea endures without me,
my live-and-let-live policy.
Lolling just out of reach
I chanted the liturgy:
You are my Origin,
Mighty One,
Source and Resource.

But the Sea's mind is too wide,
my own complains, and kicking
sand on the dozing
assembly, I turn my heel
to the order of tides;

Another year to be footloose,
to be faithless.

Roar From The Wilderness

Beauty and truth are one, said Keats.
It must be so, but must beauty be extreme-
Beheading at a party,
Gore on a silver tray?
Truth is as fitful,
You never know where to look.

That night the music was beauty,
the dancing princess,
fruit in still life,
the rousing fountains of laughter;
Truth crouched in the kitchen
ready to crash the party.

Today is my birthday,
there is no dance,
but I hold the weight of a gift-
the heavy, hair-shocked head
borne dark and dripping among us,
a roar from the wilderness
about beauty and truth.

Boundaries

Mummy-bundled, the street man
sleeps in his chaise on the church porch.
Winter's coming;
he intends to stay.

Neighbors complain to the pastor:
The man's schizo, a community splinter.
Church members sigh to each other
over life's predicaments.
The street man expels dark sounds
as he brushes his teeth in the men's room
Sunday morning
while the congregation sings
"Blest Be the Tie That Binds."

The police can do nothing
unless the church does;
The church can do nothing
because he is the neighbor
she is bound to love.

The street man loves freedom.
His feet are light, his eyes flick,
his goods balloon a wagon.
He knows the hatred of walls-
hospital, prison,
and is bound to be free.

The street man and the church
keep guard
across broken
boundaries.

Hawk

Your shadow circles.
Grass bows to the brush
of your dark pass.
The sun is too fierce,
I cannot see,
but your piercing eye pins me,
a rabbit writhing,
earth-hearted,
fearing the seizing,
the wrenching,
the bearing sun-ward.

Through A Glass, Less Darkly

He said he had enough
of overgrown shrubs
blocking the window.
He took shears,
sharp as scalpels,
and trimmed and dragged away
the tangle.

I noticed then
the dust and cobwebs,
old feathers, fly specks, storm streaks.
I filled a bucket with water,
got soap and rags,
and washed and shined
till the window vanished.

We stood to look out,
stood in the light like children,
looked at each other amazed,
gazed at the sky and blinked,
while the light
poured pure upon us
from a blue and stunning heaven.

Utterance

"May I help you?" I wait,
and you enter
the Gethsemane of speech.

Your body contorts, arms
thrash at imprisoned signals;
saliva spurts, eyes
purse with each spasmed sound.
Sweat oozes like blood
at the wrenched agony
of utterance.

I do not dare to help you.
Language makes, as it is made.
You are born, giving birth,
a haloed madonna,
the word thrust forth
throws light in your eyes.

And still you must know
the dark passion of the garden,
where swords slash at our ears,
and words echo in trees;
where life is made whole
in the lonely, laboring night.

About the Author

Barbara Joyce Esch was born on January 23, 1937 in Pigeon, Michigan. As a farm-child she was close to fields, woods, and animals, a world that continues to inspire her life and work. She wrote her first poems in her Michigan farmhouse and has written as a teenager living and going to school in Arizona and Virginia, and as a young wife and mother in Pennsylvania. She has written essays and articles as well as poetry and published in many periodicals and journals during the past twenty-five years.

The Mennonite Church has been an immeasurable influence throughout her life. She has served on pastoral ministry teams as a lay person and a licensed pastor. She is presently the chaplain to persons with developmental disabilities at Indian Creek Foundation. Her family of three grown children, daughters-in-law, three grandchildren and husband Harold are a source of gladness. She lives in Telford, Pennsylvania.